NO LONGER A PAWN

TRUE STORIES ABOUT YOUNG
PEOPLE WHO FOUND DIRECTION
AND TRUTH FOR A MEANINGFUL
LIFE AFTER BEING IN PITS OF
DESTRUCTION FOR MANY YEARS

COMPILED BY PAULA COLE

No Longer a Pawn, by Paula Cole

2023 Published in the United States

All rights reserved. Nothing is to be copied. Only small quotes may be made citing the work and the author.

All scripture quotations, unless otherwise marked, are taken from the *New King James Version*, (NKJV). Copyright© 1982 by Thomas Nelson, Inc. Used by permission. All rights reserved.

Scripture quotations marked (KJV), are taken from the *King James Version*. All rights reserved.

Scripture quotations marked (NLT), are from *the Holy Bible,* New Living Translation, copyright © 1996, 2004, 2007. Used by permission of Tyndale House Publishers, Inc., Carol Stream, IL. 60189. All rights reserved.

"Scriptures quotations taken from the Amplified Bible (AMPC), Copyright © 1954,1958, 1962, 1964, 1965, 1987 by The Lockman Foundation. Used by permission. www.lockman.org"

Cover photo from iStock.com/Lexx

Chapter heading image from iStock.com/Lora-Sutyagina

Cover design by Tiffany Cole

ISBN 978-0-9747092-2-2

TABLE OF CONTENTS

FORWARD	2
INTRODUCTION	5
PSALM 107:10-16	8
PEOPLE DO THINGS FOR A REASON	9
CHILD OF LIGHT COVERED WITH SHAME	15
MIRROR, MIRROR ON THE WALL, I AM MY FATHER AFTER ALL	21
A SON OF DISOBEDIENCE	26
WHEN YOU HAVE NO WORTH	32
LOWEST OF THE LOW	38
MY FORTY YEARS IN THE WILDERNESS	46
THE QUEST FOR TRUTH IS IN EVERY GENERATION	53
PSALM 116:1-9	58
PRAYER	59
I JOHN 1:5-10	60
ENDNOTES	61

FORWARD

IF I HAD ONLY KNOWN

In reading the stories collected in this book, I realized very quickly they were in many ways, my story. I'd like to think I would have guarded my heart and mind better, if I had been able to read such real life stories when I was a young person. Many of the choices these young people made were the result of the poor decisions made by their parents. In their own efforts to live as "grown-ups," they floundered without clear guidance or a consistent godly example. They lacked wise counsel and direction based on God's word. It showed up in their choices to follow the world and live in disobedience to God. Some did know they were choosing to sin. They desired to live out their "free will" by what seemed right in their own eyes.

I was raised by very godly parents. I accepted Christ Jesus when I was very young and I consistently sought to live for Him. As an adult with a family, I found myself compromising by allowing things in my life that separated me from God and a right relationship with Him.

Alcohol seemed harmless enough, until it became the normal in my family gatherings. Then there were those late night calls letting me know a loved one had been picked up for drinking and driving. The reality of my compromises came crashing down on me. I had a very real talk with God. I asked Him how to heal my family. It was as if I heard Him say out loud, "It has to begin with you!"

I realized in that moment, I had been watching the clock daily, to plan when I could have my next drink. The problem was mine and with me. I asked God for help and to take away all the desire for alcohol. He did this for me! He is so good!

God went much further by placing me within a Bible study with God-loving and God-fearing women. They loved me and held me up with prayer. With encouragement, they challenged me to be accountable to my claim I wanted to do and be what God desired. By studying His word together each week and on my own daily, God has not only restored me, but renewed my heart and mind. The things of the world are passing away, along with their hold on me.

I now work in ministry full time and He has given me such a heart for others. I know their struggles are real whatever their causes. From my own experience, I tell them God is bigger and He can deliver them from any sin they are living in.

As with the people in these stories, the darkness of the world once separated them from the light that came into the world two thousand years ago. This light will shine into a person's life when he starts seeking for something better. God will make Himself known and call each one to come unto Him when pride and self-sufficiency crumble. He can heal and restore their families and the friends around them. There is no limit to His divine saving and delivering power, and the grace He bestows to help us forgive others and ourselves. We can then know the power He gives to walk in righteousness and begin to take on the likeness of Christ.

I am encouraged by these words from the Bible in the book of I John, chapter 1:

4"We are writing these things that you may fully share our joy. 2This one who is life itself was reveled to us, and we have seen him. And now we testify and proclaim to you that he is the one who is eternal life. He was with the Father, and then he was reveled to us. 5This is the message we have heard from him (Jesus) and now declare to you: 'God is light, and there is no darkness in him at all.'"
(NLT)

Through His mighty word, He guides us and with His Spirit, He leads us. He sent Jesus Christ, His only Son, to die that we might have life, now and forever more. To Him alone, is all our praise!

Lindy Coughlin,
Overcomers' Coach

INTRODUCTION

THE BATTLE FOR YOU

Did you know there is a battle raging for your life, even as you read these words? The battle is between the forces of good and evil; it is a spiritual battle. The key warriors are Jesus Christ and Satan, the devil himself. Jesus is the Son of God who died to cancel your sins and give you life. Satan's sole purpose on the other hand, is to steal, kill and destroy all those who the heavenly Father loves, namely you.

There are times when all of us can be caught up by these forces that are stronger than our ability to perceive them. Most often the evil forces (whether we believe in evil or not) are in play on the heels of rebellion and disobedience to God and our parents. We are spiritually blind and insensitive to the deceptions that come through the voices of others, especially those in the media and social web. By making foul choices, we begin our journey away from God. If we choose to stay on His narrow path, we will reap good and the gift of life found in Jesus.

Out of Jesus' path of life, we are all in Satan's territory where he directs our steps much like a pawn on a chessboard. As pawns, most people are considered to be insignificant players, something that he can use to reach his purposes. They can be easily wiped out or end up impoverished in pits of destruction. Their lives are largely wasted and lived without much good or happiness coming to them.

Although some men have great riches and seem to live as kings, they are still pawns on the devil's chessboard. Their lives are lying examples of supposed blessing to the rest of the world. God is just. He promises to balance the scales. The riches they enjoy now are all they will ever have. At the end of days, all will see their poverty of soul.

In the following stories, you will read how young people became entangled on the slippery slopes of destruction. Their choices seemed right to them, but friends or an absentee, apathetic or abusive father helped set the stage for their downfall. For all, it wasn't until they cried out in humility and repentance to Jesus, that their lives turned around. He cleansed them of guilt and shame, and removed them from Satan's clutches. No longer were they caught in a deadly game.

Where are you in this battle for life and death? Let the sense of urgency allow the Holy Spirit of God to work in your soul. He has made every provision for you to have a new Spirit-filled life, but He will not force you to choose His way.

Someone may say they came to Jesus and asked Him to forgive them of their sins, but they did not have a change of heart with peace. Becoming a true believer is not a once and done act. There is a personal need to seek Him by learning to pray and reading the Bible. His Holy Spirit may reveal there are still sinful activities which are blocking the ability to experience His full, cleansing presence. By continuing to turn to Him, a spirit of joy and peace will fill an empty heart.

There is a saying that fits into everyone's struggle when dealing with the temptations the devil presents. May you remember this as the Holy Spirit, through your conscience, attempts to turn you away from bad choices:

"Sin (and Satan) will take you down a road you never wanted to be on. It will keep you longer than you ever wanted to stay. It will cost you more than you ever wanted to pay."

Think about this as you read these stories, and see if you can tell how these young people became the pawns of Satan. Where did he take them? How long did he hold them? What did it cost them before they reached the bottom of a pit, and cried out for the rescue only Jesus could provide?

Is this really what you want for yourself?

Paula Cole

THERE IS NOTHING NEW UNDER THE SUN

Some sat in darkness and deepest gloom, imprisoned in chains of misery.
They rebelled against the word of God, scorning the counsel of the Most High.
That is why he broke them with hard labor; they fell, and no one was there to help them.
"LORD, help!" they cried in their trouble, and he saved them from their distress.
He led them from the darkness and deepest gloom; he snapped their chains.
Let them praise the LORD for his great love and the wonderful things he has done for them.
Psalm 107:10-15
New Living Translation

PEOPLE DO THINGS FOR A REASON

We humans all enter the world in the same way. Some have loving care while others are neglected, even abused. Our growth and opportunities are impacted by others and the environment around us. Apart from God's divine intervention, those like me, born in the slums of the world, in ghettos or on the other side of the tracks, come to realize at a young age our lives will be one of continual struggle. The hopelessness we live in causes us to do things where we end up in Satan's old pits of destruction. We have no hope of ever finding a way out.

I was a boy born on the wrong side of the tracks in the early 1950's in Mobile, Alabama. In those days there was a real lack of charity and welfare. The poor had to survive the best they could on their own resources and the cast off "trash" of others.

My dad married my momma when she was only thirteen; she soon had a baby girl. By the time she was sixteen, she had me. My father left us, taking my sister with him before I could remember who he was. Momma and I went to live down the dusty road with her parents. They were both handicapped, and since momma was uneducated, they could never find the money to go to court to get support from my father for my care.

When I was fairly young, Momma got a job working at a bar and she often took me with her. I'm sure I put on a show as I learned to dance to the music, which I loved. I was comfortable there. The regulars were our friends.

When I was about ten, Momma married another loser. During the summer when she went to work, he would lock me in a closet so he could go drinking with friends. In the darkness, I had lots of imaginary playmates.

Finally, after days and days in the dark, school started. But one day, boy howdy, I came home and he was bending over Momma, beating her in the face. I quickly picked up the baseball bat he had given me and knocked him out cold. I nearly killed him, but I didn't care.

Momma got herself together, and that night we hitchhiked to Houston to her sister's place. She and my uncle agreed to take me into their care and get me back in school. In a few years, he taught me to be a surveyor and by 16, I had a job with the county. With money in my pocket, I got married and it wasn't long before our first child came along. That beautiful little red-haired baby girl weighed only three and a half pounds, caught pneumonia, and her weight dropped to a little over a pound. For the first time ever, I found the floor with my knees.

My granddaddy told me years before that God was my Father--the Daddy that I never had. I had prayed once before at a girlfriend's church for Jesus to forgive me of my sins, but I never changed my ways nor prayed again. Now, in desperation I cried out to Him, "God if You are real, save my daughter!" And He did!

I began to pray more, but I was still plagued with the pain of my past. It gave rise to a wild streak that got me into trouble with the law. After my son was born, I decided to go into the army so I could learn more to provide for my family and not be home fighting with my wife. My inlaws, who didn't like me and my long hair, took the opportunity to persuade her to get a divorce, shattering my hopes and dreams for a better life.

Once out of the service, I had no place to go. I met a nice woman; we married and had three girls. We even started going to a little country church. God was really working in my heart. People said they could see a change in me; even the lines of my wrinkled face seemed to soften, and I had a smile once in a while instead of a scowl. I met a couple who treated us as real friends and had us in their home. This was something for a guy from the other side of the tracks.

One day I went to their home to work on patching the roof. While taking a break, the lady and I got to talking about sin in our lives. She said her sins were mostly different than mine, but the difference between us was really quite small compared to our sin and God's holiness. We sat there and cried together over our worthlessness and the great love God showed to us by forgiving our sins. Oh what joy! I really felt accepted for the first time in my life.

Some time passed and life was definitely better until the devil got my wife's ear through a "friend." I was divorced again, but eventually vindicated from the slander and lies. However, the damage was done. Not being one to live alone, I married a woman who had two small boys. I recognized they needed a daddy. I could help and provide for them, keeping them from the heartache I had known. Twenty-eight years later, their "real" father came by, and they ran him off. They said they only had one dad—me!

During this time, I went back to playing drums for a band at a bar. I had learned about music while staying with my uncle in Houston. Now, I played for the sheer joy of talking to others who were pawns in their own pits of destruction, giving each of them words of comfort and hope.

A lovely young woman who worked in the bar was drinking much, much more than she should. One night, I asked her why she was hurting herself. She shook her head and said her baby died when she was only four months old. Then her husband left her. She had no reason to live. Here was someone doing the wrong thing for a reason.

I asked her what would make her stop. She replied that she didn't know and why did I care anyway? I asked her if she had ever heard of Jesus.

"Yeah, I heard of Him."

"Did you ever ask Him to help you?"

"No, I didn't think I was worthy. Larry, I know there is something different about you, 'cause you don't drink when you come in here. Why?"

"Well, I don't need to drink no more. Jesus took the pain out of my heart from all my past. He forgave me of all the things I have done wrong. Jesus loves you as much as He loves me. If you ask Him to be in your life and accept Him, He will be."

"Would you talk to me more about Jesus?"

"I sure will." We went outside behind the bar, and there, amongst the garbage cans and litter, I told her how much God loved her, how He sent His Son Jesus to die to take away her sins. I led her in a prayer to confess her sins. We cried, we laughed, and we thanked Jesus. When I left her, she had a new beginning with a huge smile on her face.

Unknown to us, but known to God, her future days were very short. Within the next two weeks she died of cirrhosis, a result of all her drinking that ruined her liver. God knew; He cared, and I was blessed to have been a part of helping her find forgiveness and peace of heart before she met Him.

People do bad things for a reason. Because they are poor in spirit, their sin makes them feel so hopeless and ashamed, they turn to the world to find some relief. Satan convinces them that God could never love or care for them. But God is better than the most loving mother who would not give up on her child. Just so, when God sees His child wants something better, He will not send His child away. He is fully aware of our hurts and pains, as well as those who caused them.

Because we live in a fallen world with other sinners, often we are their victims. But no matter, Jesus calls the poor in spirit, the humble, to come to Him in spite of their sins and feelings of unworthiness. God can take them out of the devil's hands, cleanse their hearts, and give them a new life of freedom and joy. They are then forever released from the sins and darkness of their past. They only have to walk in their new identity.

I don't think there was anyone as low as I was. God became the Father I never had. He picked me up out of my pit of destruction and washed away my sins because I chose to believe in Jesus. He gave me a new life that I never imagined could be mine. I have fallen many times, but He still loves me and keeps me. I am alive today because of Him.

Are you alive today because of Him? Should you be dead several times over? Jesus wants you to accept His sacrifice for your sins and become His child. This is your chance to have a new beginning and be set free from the guilt and shame of your past. Whatever your reasons for the things you have done...

God already knows, He still wants you!

CHILD OF LIGHT COVERED WITH SHAME

Maybe you are like me, a little girl born into a loving Christian home. I went to church with my family and learned about God. One Sunday morning, when I was only six years old, I realized Jesus died on the cross so my sins could be forgiven. I desired that He become my Savior and asked Him to come cleanse my heart through His Spirit. I was baptized soon after this, so others would know Jesus was now my Savior. Even at six, my heart was joyful; in an instant I knew everything I had done wrong was forgiven.

From that day, I seemed to grow like a butterfly coming out of its cocoon. My pastor answered the many questions I brought to him, and he even asked me to give my testimony about how I loved Jesus. Right away, I began to tell my friends at school about Jesus so they could have joy inside too.

But hidden behind my beaming smile, was a dark secret only two people knew—my relative and myself, and yes, God knew. That may seem like a puzzling part—why could I be forgiven for a sinful activity that had been occurring as far back as I could remember, and still was? God knew it wasn't my choice. My father never saw or suspected anything was amiss, but one day, my mother asked me about these things. I froze and said, "No!" I did not want to get him in trouble. At times, I thought it was my fault that he came to see me, so the abuse continued until I was nine or ten.

Having experienced this sexual touching and fondling, I felt myself to be older and wiser, "more mature" if you will. At the age of fifteen, I married a fine young man, but was divorced by the age of sixteen. I then ran far from God and my family. Being wise in my own eyes, I rented an apartment and started singing in night clubs. I threw off all restraints and partied and slept around from one person to the next.

The sinfulness of my abuser bore its fruit in me. I was looking for real love, but I only found more heartache. I had been and was now still a pawn. My heavenly Father seemed so far away, but in truth, I was never out of His reach. I was His child and He loved me, but I had lost my way on the path of life. I was now stuck in Satan's pit, deeply caked in mud, and I had no idea how to get out.

One night a nice looking man came into the club where I was singing. Not being shy, I went over to meet him. Within a few weeks we started living together and then got married two years later. He was a fireman with a steady job, so it seemed right to start a family. I developed this desperate desire to have a baby to love. I wasn't really paying much attention to God, but I did start praying to have a baby and after some time, I was finally pregnant. I was so excited!

Then the unthinkable happened; I lost the one thing that controlled my hopes for future happiness. I suffered the pain of a miscarriage, and I blamed it on God. I thought He had played a very bad trick on me. I became so bitter toward Him, it took control of my attitude and within six months I had destroyed my marriage. My bitterness had an effect on everyone around me, causing much heartache.

I left my husband, got my own apartment and settled in. I did not have a plan, but God did. By myself, I was lonely and sleepless. At the "mature" age of twenty-three, I was also broken and hopeless; I cried out to Him for help. For the first time in years, I listened and heard Him speak to my heart. He asked softly, "Are you ready to do life My way?"

My response was a desperate, "Yes!"

But then He said something I did not expect, nor did I want to hear; "Go home, Lucy!"

"What? I don't love him anymore. How will that help anything?"

With the voice of a stern Father, I again heard Him say, "Go home. I didn't ask you what you wanted. Your way has gotten you into this mess. If you are ready to truly follow Me, then you will OBEY ME, TRUST ME, and GO HOME."

On my knees, I bowed my heart and will to God in surrender. The anxiety that had been my constant burden left me. I said out loud, "Be anxious for nothing; but in everything by prayer and supplication, with thanksgiving, let your requests be made known to God. And the peace of God which passes all understanding, will guard your hearts and minds in Christ Jesus." (Philippians 4:6, 7)

If we pray and give thanks to God for the goodness He has already shown to us, He will hear us and replace the anxiety with His peace. His love for us is hard to grasp, and His ways of working far exceed our imagination. So, with this prayer, I crawled back up into bed and slept calmly and peacefully all night.

Early the next day, I found myself on the road home. My husband was shocked to see me. Without any feeling, I told him God had told me to come home. I even told him at this point I didn't love him, but if he would have me, I would return. He only nodded his head yes in affirmation. This had to be God's doing. He helped me haul all my stuff back to the house, and we tried to return to normal under these very awkward circumstances.

My husband didn't know what to expect when I started studying my Bible every day. He had never seen me do this before. Three weeks went by, and I was impatient for something to change. God caught me by surprise as He said to my mind, "Don't put time limits on Me!" Again, I was guilty of wanting to do things my way.

One day my husband came into the house, all excited about something funny that had just happened. He got me laughing just as he had done when we first met, and I fell in love with him. We fell into each other's arms and our laughter turned into tears. We held each other tight, and our tears flowed uncontrollably. Breaking through the pain, discouragement, loneliness, and bitterness, a flood of love came surging through my heart. This love was not just a love for my husband; this love was greater, and I could not comprehend it all.

God showed me I had never stopped loving my husband; I just couldn't feel it any more. So many layers of sin and heartache were buried in my heart. Worst of all, I heard the Lord say:

> "You replaced your need for Me all these years with other things and other people. If you had a baby, it would have been one more thing to separate us. I love you too much to allow that to happen. The extra love you feel is not your own, it is Mine. I love you and I want you to receive My love and forgiveness."

Wow! That day I fell in love with my Lord Jesus Christ, and I couldn't get enough of Him. He helped me to understand His plan. Even though I had a miscarriage and lost my baby, I was not under condemnation for in scripture it says, **"There is no condemnation to those who are in Christ Jesus."** (Romans 8:1)

When we come to Jesus for the forgiveness of our sins, we are really entering into His Life. "In Him, we can be assured and know that God can work all things together into a plan for good to and for those who love Him and are called according to His design and purpose." (Romans 8:28 NLT)

After a few years of learning to trust God, my marriage was completely restored. I had learned to surrender to the Lord's will, and watch Him direct my husband's steps. During that time, we had a baby girl who brought us much joy. My husband also decided to believe in Jesus. He received the cleansing of his sins through the blood of the sacrifice Jesus made for us all. To add to our joy, we had a baby boy, another of God's blessings.

I, who had lost everything as a pawn of Satan, now had a heart full of love for God, and arms of love all around me. This was the beginning of an incredible life of total sweet surrender to my Heavenly Father and Savior, who freed me from my past.

He lives in me as I reach out to others. My prayer is that anyone who reads my story may also know the joy of having all their mistakes washed away and a fresh, new life in Christ that is worth living. God alone can take a worthless, broken life, and make it into something beautiful. Admitting sin may seem hard, but every new journey starts with a first step. May you hear His call in your heart and take the first step toward Him. He will meet you.

Revelation 3:19, 20 says, "I, Jesus Christ, correct and discipline everyone I love. So be diligent and turn from your indifference. Look! I stand at the door and knock. If you hear My voice and open the door, I will come in, and we will share a meal together as friends." (NLT)

MIRROR MIRROR, ON THE WALL, I AM MY FATHER AFTER ALL

Have you ever fought for the honor of your mom or dad? Do you think they are pretty good parents, or do you wonder sometimes about the things they do? Have you ever wished you lived somewhere else? These are tough questions for any child to think about or face. It took me a long time to realize, that the so-called "fun" that my family had, brought lots of heartache with it.

Growing up, my family seemed secure. My parents got married when they were only 18, and my dad always acted like he was "happy." He would sing and be silly as the center of attention in the frequent parties at our house. In my childish eyes, it was a very entertaining environment.

However, when I was 12, my world blew apart. My father walked out one day and seldom returned. He decided that he needed a bottle of alcohol more than he needed his family. My mother had to start working, while my teenage brother and sister were busy going places with their own friends; most of the time I was left at home by myself.

One summer, I went to church camp with a friend who lived close by. I had the best time ever, and I asked Jesus to forgive me of my sins and live in my heart. I had great peace for awhile and went to church with her. It was a way to escape the emptiness at my house. Without help to show me how to grow in my relationship with Him, I soon drifted away.

Then, when I was 17, my mother left me on my own even though I had started working as soon as I could to help support myself. I stayed with friends, worked, and partied. I had watched my father do that for years, so I really thought it was the way to be happy and have friends.

I met this guy I thought was wonderful. We partied together and then married when I was twenty-two. But for some reason in his mind, I soon became a stupid person and he said I would never amount to anything. Six years later a kind woman came into my life and encouraged "stupid" me to go to college. This was such a contrast to my husband's treatment. I finished college in three years and entered the corporate world. My husband left me, and I was free.

But what is freedom if you don't know how to handle it? I soon had money to spend and found that alcohol was a big part of the work scene. Drinks at lunch or dinner and parties on the weekend, what more could a single girl want? My life was soon all about having fun and "Party" became my middle name.

Being alone was not my cup of tea, so I married again. This time I found myself in an even more abusive relationship than before. We would play happy at parties, but at home there was always turmoil and many tears.

After six years of this disorder, I had a miscarriage. He was happy about it and left me alone on Christmas Eve. That night, as I rested on my bed, I thought back on all the choices that had brought me to this place in my life. Quietly, as I was being still, peace swept over me. I now understand it was the Holy Spirit of God. His presence was real, and I knew I was not alone. I filed for divorce a few days later. It was time for a fresh start, but I could not shake my old lifestyle.

Single again, I bought a house with a nice pool. I still had a good job, so I had plenty of people and booze around on the weekends. This was the only life I knew. I was an alcoholic, but never realized it. I just wanted to have fun with my friends; in all honesty, I was empty inside.

One day, my neighbor had some tree trimmers working in his yard, and I asked if anyone could come help me. They sent over a handsome single man who cut down several branches from a tree, upsetting a small squirrel's nest with a baby inside. He managed to get the baby squirrel back in the nest and set it upright. I called him, "My hero."

He was so kind. We talked a little, and he told me his name. We went out the next week, and the next, and were married two months later.

After two bad marriages, one might wonder how I could marry again. A friend encouraged me to give him a chance. He had nothing to offer but himself; no money, no car, nothing but a working man. He had recovered from his own battle with drugs. There was something special about him.

I think God saw two single people who could be better together for Him. We were not whole in our minds, wills, or emotions. We started going to church with his brother and professed to be followers of Christ and were baptized, but you know, some of the old sins just hung on.

Finally, we realized God didn't want our lives centered around a bottle. He had more for us, and so together we decided to stop drinking. My husband was very supportive of me. I didn't really know who I was apart from alcohol. It took almost two years for me to be able to talk to people in pleasant conversation, not trash talk.

We moved from the city to start a new life away from the old haunts. It is hard to learn to walk with Jesus when old friends are trying to pull you backwards; just one more party they say.

As we began to make these changes, I met a woman who helped me learn to listen to and trust Jesus in a much closer relationship than I had ever known before. Today, I am happy, with no regrets. Jesus has taken away the heartache of my past! His love is mine forever, along with the great husband He gave me. He has also restored some broken relationships, especially the one with my mother. (She is now in love with Jesus, too.) My joy is full!

If you are looking to alcohol to get you through the day or night, or just drowning your sorrows, I can tell you there is a better way. Thirty years of my life was wasted because I chose to look at life through the bottom of a bottle. Without realizing it, I was the devil's pawn under a generational curse from my father. Maybe he was also under the same curse from his father and didn't know it.

If you are truly addicted, you have to admit it. You may think that leaving off alcohol will take all the "fun" out of your life, but you are not being honest with yourself. Those who drink regularly, only get past the shame of what they did one night, by having more drinks the next.

And if you are like most alcoholics, they may be the life of the party scene, but at home they are mean, just plain jerks. I was mean to my new husband, but thanks be to God, he didn't throw me out before God started cleaning me up! Believe me when I say, alcohol and parties get you nowhere. Jesus is the real thing and with Him, you have a new identity with a meaningful life; what everyone wants.

My favorite verse is in Psalm 142. At the beginning it says:
"I cry out to the Lord with my voice; with my voice to the Lord I make my supplication. I pour out my complaint before Him; I declare before Him my trouble." Then in verse 7 it says, **"Bring my soul out of prison, that I may praise Your name."**

God will hear YOU, if you cry out to Him today.

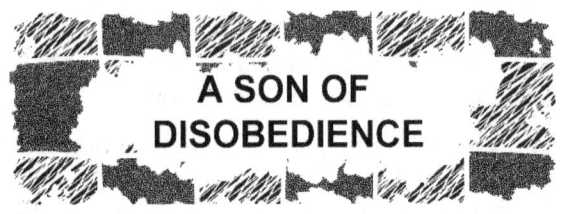

A SON OF DISOBEDIENCE

In the Bible, which is God's Holy Word, instructions for living a meaningful life are written down for all people. When understood and obeyed, God the Father can fill any life with goodness and blessing. However, there is a part of the human will that causes individuals to think they know what is best for their own life. Unknowingly, Satan is behind any choice to ignore God and His ways. As a result, a person can set out to prove that his own choices are right and good. Where does he land? Right in the darkest pit, wondering how his well-intentioned plans went so wrong. He had blindly allowed the lies of Satan to be his guide! This happened to me after I had been richly blessed.

When I was born, I was considered a miracle baby. Years before, my mother had surgery to prevent a pregnancy, so everyone was surprised to find out she was expecting. My mom and dad had each been married before, and I had older siblings from those marriages, but I felt like an only child. Our home was stable, and we went to church often, but that doesn't mean I was always following the Lord when I was older.

Around the time I was six years old, I wanted to see if God would really answer my prayers. There was a little wishing well up the street from my house and I closed my eyes and said, "Lord, You say in Your Word for us to ask and we will receive. Well, I want that Thunder Cat Car I saw on T.V."

I remember guarding that moment with the utmost secrecy and really forgot about it. When I was asked what I would like for Christmas, I requested a Nintendo which was all the rage that year.

Christmas morning finally came and I remembered about the toy I asked God for. My anticipation grew as I was opening my presents. I really surprised my parents when I barely acknowledged my new Nintendo, and just kept opening things without much apparent delight. Finally, I opened a small box and there it was; I excitedly yelled to God, "You did it! You did it! You got me the Thunder Cat Car!" My parents were dumbfounded and asked me to explain. I told them my story, and they were amazed at how God had led them to even buy the car. He worked through them to begin my relationship with the unseen God of the Bible.

Another special event in my life, as I learned that God was real, was on a trip to Sunshine Lake. I wanted to go fishing, but Dad said no because there was no bait. Mom got my rod out just so I could try. Before I dropped my line in the water, I said, "Lord, please help me catch a fish." Within thirty seconds, I had a fish. I pulled in many little perch as Dad worked quickly to get them off the line. That night, he taught me how to clean fish as he told me the story of Jesus telling the disciples that He would answer their prayers. They simply needed to believe and not doubt as they prayed. (Mark 11:23, 24) This helped to cement the reality of God in my mind.

My family told of these events for years, speaking of the faith of a child. However, it made me too self-assured, that whatever I wanted, God was going to bless. I did not fully know Him, nor was I listening for the wisdom of the Holy Spirit to direct my steps.

When I was fifteen, my grandfather took me for a ride in his little Cessna, as he often did. He offered to pay for my college education if I would stop having girl friends until I graduated. That sounded good to me, so I broke up with my girlfriend of several years and began thinking about college. This focus only lasted three weeks!

One morning as I headed down through a creek area to the practice field, I saw a girl sitting Indian style off in the distance. I went to see what she was doing and as I approached her, I thought I heard the Lord say, "She is going to be your wife; love her as I have loved you!" We began hanging out together. I told my parents and they reminded me of my grandfather's offer, but I said I would choose God's plan for my life, whatever that might be. They said God would work it out if it was meant to be. We were married the next year and lived with her parents. It took many years for me to learn to love her as I felt God loved me.

Once married, I had to have a job. A judge gave me papers so that I could go to work while I was still in school. After reaching graduation, the insurance would not pay for my Ritalin prescription. I started using speed, which seemed to help me be my "normal" self. However, along with smoking and drinking, I became a total wreck. In desperation, I cried out to God and in time, He delivered me from the taste and desire for these things. He blessed me with a job in the oil field. I earned enough money to pay off my house and land. After 22 years of marriage, I was of one heart and mind with my wife, who had come to love the Lord with me. We also had two great kids. What more could a man want? Then disaster struck!!

One night about midnight, I woke up to find my wife sitting up in bed. I nudged her and told her to lie down, but she didn't move. I laid her back down on the bed and did CPR that I had just learned to do at work. I got her heart going, but at the hospital, it became clear her brain had been without oxygen for too long. With the agreement of her family, we took her off life support and donated her organs. I left the hospital and relapsed on speed that started the downward spiral that left my life in ashes. Everything in my life was burned up because I drank judgment and condemnation on myself.

Before long, I ended up in prison for drinking and driving. I was in a truck, racing down a highway, when I missed a newly placed stoplight and hit a car broadside. I nearly killed the driver. The DA wanted to send me to prison for 18 years. My lawyer said it looked bad.

The Lord spoke to me to put my life in the hands of the lady I hit. What would be a good sentence for me in her mind since she had suffered so very much? As it turned out, she was a Christian and God gave her a dream of sentencing me to only four years! The judge accepted her sentence. Later that year, God completely healed her for her obedience.

In prison, God spoke to me and showed me my walk with Him was up and down because I didn't really "fear Him." That is, I didn't have a true respect or awareness of His holiness and what He desired of those who followed Him. Without meaning to, I was rather casual in my approach to Him, even as I had been as a child. I circled all the words in my Bible that had to do with death and fear. In Proverbs 1:7, I found, "The reverent and worshipful fear of the Lord is the beginning and the principal and choice part of knowledge [its starting point and its essence]; but fools despise skillful and godly Wisdom, instruction and discipline." (AMPC)

That last part was me. I had become a disobedient son of God, not listening to godly wisdom! My heavenly Father had to bring me to a full stop in my foolish ways before I killed myself or someone else. I served time in prison and then alcohol rehab, which was a lesson in itself. Finally, I was able to go to Calvary Commission in Lindale, Texas, and spent a year under their discipleship and Bible School training program.

Learning to die to yourself and your foolish ways of thinking is very difficult. We all want to be right, but when we are not, it is extremely hard to admit we are wrong. This makes it even more difficult to bend our knees before God and admit we are a sinner in need of a Savior. In Luke 9:23, Jesus says, "If any man will come after Me, let him deny himself, and take up his cross daily, and follow Me."

What does this mean? Everyday there are things we want to do to gratify ourselves. We have plans and work that we want done in a certain way. Often, uncooperative people, interruptions, and other things happen to totally frustrate and block what we set out to accomplish. How we handle this, is what Jesus is referring to as "taking up your cross." The cross is a place of death; we have to turn from our desires and toward His. He may set us on a different path that helps us release our expectations and put us in the place of helping others instead.

If things are not working out as expected, letting go and remembering God is in control can be really tough. Maybe our activity is not what He wants. Right then, there is the need to bend our heads and seriously say to Him:

"Yes Lord, Your will be done. Help me accept Your plan for my day and whatever You bring into my path. I am willing for Your will to be done even though I am hurting, confused, and disappointed. I surrender to You. Please forgive me for trying to run the show to please myself."

You love Him most when you can say from your heart, "Your will, not mine." Then you know without a doubt you are His, and He will work situations out for your good to His praise and glory.

WHEN YOU HAVE NO WORTH

Once upon a time. . . .Well yes, once upon a time I came into this world as the second child of my mom and dad, but it was no fairy tale being in our family. Dad also had two children from a previous marriage, and eventually they had three more children. A whole brood of us were cooped up in an apartment, and I was the very middle child.

My dad worked at a plant where they made the rubber for tires. It was a dirty job, and he didn't make much money. We lived in government housing with other minorities all around us. This was an advantage to me, for it had a positive influence on all my later relationships.

When I was about eight years old, we moved to another state where my granny lived. One night my sister and I stayed with a friend, and when we returned home the next day, everything in the house was in total disarray. My parents had a fight to end all fights. Dad left, breaking my heart. Not long afterwards, he flipped his truck and was in ICU for months. When he got out of the hospital, he stayed at Granny's. My siblings and I would go there to take care of him. It gave me a little purpose and satisfaction to know I was "helping."

Left with five children to take care of on her own, my mom decided she no longer wanted a straight life. She had already helped raise three brothers while her mother worked two to three jobs because her dad was an alcoholic. She decided to make our mobile home a party place. Sometimes there were at least twenty people sleeping everywhere. Some girls brought their babies along with them. I never wanted a doll for Christmas because I always had a real baby to carry around.

When I was in the fourth grade, I remember asking when I was going back to school. I was told there was "no school." I wondered why my teacher gave me homework to do if I didn't have to take it back. It didn't seem to matter to anyone.

The young women staying at the house took care of us while Mom was out stealing. Her big thing was to swipe and forge checks. She eventually was in and out of prison, and I went to live with my dad at his place. He had money from being disabled and from having many dependent children, but a lot of it went into drugs. I don't remember all the utilities being on at the same time very often. Granny brought us food. She kept us alive. Sometimes she would take us to Vacation Bible School, but I knew very little about God except for the cussing I heard around me.

Because of this, I became a party girl too. At thirteen, I had a twenty-three year old boy friend. I was looking for love and someone to care for me, but I had no wisdom and no direction.

At fourteen, when another guy came along who took me to Dairy Queen, bought me a meal, and gave me a little pot, I thought he had to be "the one." I desired to be with him A-L-L the time. He tried to get me to go to school, but I wouldn't have it. I was pregnant and just wanted him.

We moved to Dallas, where he was a drug dealer, and I became his punching bag for the next eight years. I had a second child and then in no time, I was pregnant again. I knew he would kill me for it. For the first time, I really prayed and asked God what I should do. I decided to move back home.

I sought out a place to have a pregnancy test. Once it was confirmed, I asked the lady where I could get an abortion. Her answer rings in my ears to this day, "Why do you ladies never give the third baby a chance for life?"

I had the abortion back in Dallas anyway, and was in such pain afterwards, I was put on medication. Knowing life with the father of my two children was not going to get better, I loaded my car with their things one day and left with them in tow. In only a month, he came to take them back. He had their birth certificates and shot records; I did not have a court order enabling me to keep them.

For the next 15 years, I worked at a sandwich place. I enjoyed meeting people, but I could not break away from the only way of life I knew. Soon, I started doing some drugs and going to a bar. There are always lots of single men on hand looking for a woman who doesn't think much of herself. I met an older man that I thought was really nice. He bought me roses one day and then brought me lunch several times, and I ended up pregnant again. When I told him, he rebuffed me and said he wasn't the father. He was lying, but I couldn't prove it. What was I to do?

Two of my friends said they would stand beside me whatever I chose to do. I had nothing to offer a baby; no home, nothing. I chose to have another abortion, not knowing the soul pain that would eventually arise. I could not run from the pain or get it out of my mind.

I returned to my party life but got caught with some drugs. I was to be in jail for 20 days, but because I had no record and the jail was overcrowded, I was out in only five. Thinking I was bullet proof, I took the blame for an incident in a government assisted housing project, so my friend wouldn't get evicted. I ended up in jail for 24 months. That was more than a slap on the wrist. My first probation officer was very strict and expected me to do all he said and when! He was slowing me down. The second man was very kind and as my mind was clearing, I realized I did not want to continue in the life I had known.

A loving woman I call "Mom" was taking care of my brother who was mentally challenged, while my real mother was in prison. Sitting at her home one day with her friends, I realized she had the life I wanted and needed. I listened to her talk of the good and blessings from God that filled her life. She invited me to a Bible study she was attending and then we went on a retreat together.

A month before the retreat, we were asked to put a rock in our purses to represent the things that were dragging us down. I had a load—drugs, guys, TWO ABORTIONS stood out. I began asking for God's forgiveness. The grief in me was great, knowing I had willingly killed two precious souls that were His.

One night at the retreat, there was a cross standing in front of the group. As the speaker was relating how she overcame sin in her life, and received the forgiveness God wanted to give us all, I finally began to realize He was forgiving me. There was no need for me to carry my burden any longer. I put all my stones at the foot of the cross and prayed to have the spirit of negativity and grief lifted off my shoulders.

I was free. I didn't need to carry the weight of my sinful past any longer. I was not a child of the devil, as some wanted to believe, but a new child of God, totally forgiven of every sin of my past. The bondage to the sinful living I was in, and the baggage I carried, were no longer mine.

To my surprise, I woke up the next morning, and my cigarettes didn't taste good. I was pregnant again, having fallen into the "nice guy" trap not too long before. This time it was different. I had feelings for the father, but knew not to marry him. We are friends and share her bills. She is "my forgiveness baby, a second chance." She has brought us both so much joy.

I was baptized, and several women have spoken to me that I am a woman of "worth." I am worthy because the blood of Jesus has cleansed me of all my sins, abortions and all. Jesus died for me that I might walk in a new life. Serving Him is not a problem because I know He loves me so much. I still make mistakes and do some things wrong, but I know to ask for His forgiveness right away.

God provided a good lawyer who helped me get custody of my older children. We are happy together. I have my own place for us to live, and am working in my church where I can sense God's presence all the time. And He has said, "I know the thoughts that I think toward you, not for evil but for good, to give you a future and a hope." (Jer 29:11)

I praise Him for His great mercy to me. There is no good reason to wait to be set free from the load you carry. There is no good reason to continue to hate yourself any longer. His mercy is available to anyone who will humbly come to Him and ask for their sins to be forgiven. Of all the things God does, He WAITS to show His love and mercy to us. How long has He been waiting to show you?

LOWEST OF THE LOW

Meningitis! How did my baby get meningitis? Certainly my mother must have been extremely upset and scared when the doctor diagnosed my illness as spinal meningitis when I was just a small baby. The doctor told my mother I would probably have sight and hearing loss among other issues. Mother, however, was praying for me; I recovered and these problems never materialized. God fully healed me.

At the age of four, while playing with a friend out in the front yard, a man pulled up in his car and was about to abduct us. Right then, my friend's father opened the garage door, sending the abductor speeding away. Again, God had seen to my protection. He certainly loved me, but I didn't recognize His hand at work in my life. Though I knew about these events in my childhood, I never made any connection to them when I was older; I did not remind myself He was someone who I could cry out to when my heart was breaking.

My biological father left my mother when I was very young. My older sister and I stayed with our grandparents much of the time while mother worked several jobs. When I was about six, she remarried, and for the first time I had a father figure in my life that I could refer to as "Dad." However, their marriage only lasted seven years, ending in devastation for all.

At the ages of thirteen and fifteen, my sister and I were insecure and angry. We were on our own much of the time while mother was working. We began running around with a crowd of teens and adults who were into alcohol, pot and other substances. We felt a great pressure to feel loved and to belong to the group. Our defenses fell to the ground as we caved in to their destructive influences.

We continued to go to church, and mother read her Bible and set the right example. She tried to protect our ears and eyes and put God's word in our heads, but it did no good. We had become very rebellious. The men in our lives who had called themselves "Christians," had let us down. We didn't want to do anything God's way; we thought we knew better.

The world Satan offered was very enticing. Like pawns on a chessboard, the enemy moved people in and out of our lives as we started looking for someone to love and care for us. Our real father was an alcoholic and his life was in shambles. He was not someone we could depend on, but we never saw his alcohol problems as a picture of our future selves.

The years from fourteen to sixteen were really tough years for me. I tried to run away and suffered with bulimia. My mother had her own problems; I didn't want to burden her. With no one to whom I felt safe to share my pain, I was miserable. Getting caught with drugs and skipping school landed me in a juvenile detention program which helped me at least finish school. At fifteen, I was "in love" with a guy and lost my virginity. He left shortly thereafter; I was just his pawn, his play thing, one among many to whom he had fed his phony lines.

Before long, I began "dating" again; only this time I became pregnant. I tried to deny it and kept partying. After four months, I knew for sure I was carrying a child. I knew abortion was wrong, so instead, I secretly hoped I would have a miscarriage so I could be free to be me.

Thankfully, my son was born healthy and I loved him greatly. We were together all the time, attached at the hip; life was hard, very hard. Because I had no good sense or discernment about young men, I kept seeing my son's dad. Before long, I became pregnant again. My mother was livid. How were we going to support these two babies? I was still so young and the father was less than responsible. He actually was arrested with a truckload of marijuana at the border.

After a while, I started seeing another guy my age that I had known in seventh grade. We met up again at church. Since his parents were members there, I thought he was from a good home and would be a good guy to hang out with. I did not recognize any warning signs that this was not true. I was only concerned about having fun.

One day I entered a drawing and won a free night's stay at a local hotel. I called my friends to come to a party for the evening. Everything was all set, except for the care of my children.

In an effort to show me tough love, my mother refused to take care of my children while I was out partying again. I knew having them with me at the hotel was not the best plan, but I believed I had no other options. A friend helped me keep an eye on them, and they finally went to sleep on one of the beds. As the night progressed, we had our drinks as always. My boy friend was acting strange, but I just assumed it was because he was as drunk as I was. I finally passed out; the rest of the night was a blur.

The next morning my mother and grandfather came knocking at the hotel room door to take the babies to breakfast. Though hung over, I got them up in the dark and sent them with my mother. In no time she came back, very upset and emotional. She turned on the lights to show me that someone had beaten my nineteen month-old son. He had wounds and bruises from his face to his feet.

I was in shock, confused and baffled! How could this have happened? The police came and arrested my boyfriend. CPS met my mother at the hospital, and they interrogated and accused me of this horror. Rubbing my son's wounds in my face, they gave my mother sole custody. During the entire course of the ongoing investigation, I was only allowed to see my children with supervised visits.

If you were to ask me when the darkest time of my life was, it would definitely have been right then. Shame, guilt, unworthiness, tormenting thoughts, and mental anguish all came crashing in on me. I was nothing. I had nothing—no children, no home, and my car broke down on this very day! I felt totally undeserving of anything good, and I just wanted to be numb. **I was at the lowest of the low**.

In time, they declared me innocent of any abuse, and I was able to see my children and have them with me, but my mother still had full custody. For many months, she had control over every time I was with my children.

After experiencing such a grievous situation, I would like to say that I became more responsible, but I continued to drink even when I had my children with me and while I was driving.

Oftentimes, the police stopped me and issued me several DWIs. I was on probation and I moved in with various men as their "common law" wife. This was the only life I seemed to know. I could not get off the merry-go-round of pain and addiction. I continued to be a pawn playing the devil's game. I was spiraling downward and taking my children with me.

Finally, I married a man who had two young daughters, and I settled down. He helped me fight for the right to have my children with me without my mother's interference. Life was good and after nearly eleven years together, we had a son. His girls were now teenagers and had some issues about me I could not resolve. When our son was only four months old, they manipulated a situation that cast me in a very bad light. They brought charges against me and I was hauled off to jail, as my daughter, who had come for a visit, looked on in unbelief. My husband believed his daughters, so once again I was divorced and left with nothing.

Wrecked repeatedly with feelings of anxiety, failure, unworthiness, and shame, I cried out to God. I tried to quit drinking so that I could be a good example for my daughter. I did not want to lose her too. I tried exercising to relieve the depression, but in no time, I was back at the club scene. These are Satan's dens for anyone full of heartache and low self esteem. There are plenty of people who will listen to your tale of woe and offer you Satan's best, worldly advice.

I met Ken there. His kindness drew me to him. I had no desire for a relationship with him, but my life needed a little kindness. We ended up renting a small place. My daughter and I started going to school and both of us were working. I was attending church and was desperately looking for fulfillment by trying to put my life together and to show that I could be successful. God was there, but I didn't recognize His hand moving in my affairs.

In time, I decided to move to another city where I could see my youngest son more often. I got a good job as a dental assistant, so I decided to buy a house. However, that financial burden only added to my stress. After a short while, I decided the only way I could make the payments was to let Ken move his own RV onto the property and "pay rent." This worked for awhile, however I knew this was not the way God wanted me to live. We agreed to end our physical relationship. God helped me with all my financial struggles.

I had a friend who owned a guitar shop nearby. That guitar shop became my refuge from fear and being alone. Sometimes he prayed over me, or I just sat and relaxed. Through listening to worship music, reading and meditating on my Bible, I was able to stop drinking any alcohol and started spending more time with Jesus. As I cried out to Him, my anxiety began to fade and I could live life in peace once again. How long had it been?

For the nearly twenty years or more spanning my young life, I battled with alcohol and the hurt of abandonment by the so-called "Dads" in my life. Satan was quick to take advantage of my pain and add to it. As his pawn, he led me down the world's path of alcohol, drugs and sex—all in my effort to find real love. He certainly was behind every false step, trying to destroy my life.

The world can never supply true happiness or love; those only come from the heart of God. He is the source of all that is truly love.

When we ask God to forgive us of our sins, He alone can fill our emptiness and remove our feelings of nothingness. His redeeming love can bring restoration to relationships that were broken by our sinfulness. After eating and living on the dregs of Satan's best for so long, I marvel at the mystery of how God can give us a taste of heaven here on earth. The good things on earth however, are all those who reject Christ will ever receive or know. The blessings and joys of heaven are waiting for those who truly love and believe in Jesus.

Grace is God's favor and blessing poured out upon us. We don't deserve it and can do nothing to earn it. There are challenges to be sure, for new relationships are always clouded by those in our past. It is very hard not to allow our baggage of pain and rejection to color the way we respond to others in new situations.

If I had sought God in those years after I was hurt so badly, I could have known how much He valued me and loved me. My life would have been so different. But He does not condemn me for those wasted years. He has used them instead to make my life shine into the darkness of other hurting souls. He can take the broken and damaged lives that Satan has worn down, and fill their hearts and spirits with unimaginable joy.

From the Bible I know "not to worry about anything; instead pray about everything. Tell God what you need and thank Him for all He has done. Then you will have God's peace...which will guard your heart and mind as you live in Christ Jesus." Philippians 4:6, 7 (NLT)

MY 40 YEARS IN THE WILDERNESS

Do you remember much from when you were two years old? Most of us don't. Our earliest memories most often are from when we were at least three. This is a good thing for me, for there was a lot of trauma in my early life and I can't remember any one incident. I do think I suffered emotional scars from the turmoil around me that caused my father to leave my mother when I was only two. They were both alcoholics, but she was in such bad shape she could not take care of herself or anyone else. My father decided to take a job in another state over 2000 miles away. One day, he bundled me and my sister up with our things and loaded us into his car. It could not have been a pleasant time for any of us. My sister was a little older. She probably understood we were leaving our mother.

As a single dad, my father provided the best he could for us. He kept a roof over our heads and kept us fed. I never was close to him though; he was so unpredictable. I never knew how he would respond to me at any time.

When I was fourteen, he told me I would need to get a job if I wanted any new school clothes. My buddy and I got jobs at a liquor store. In retrospect, this was the last place I needed to be as the son of an alcoholic. Satan certainly understood the family weakness for alcohol, so he directed my steps to this place; I could drink and make some money too! What more could a teenage boy want?

Our job was to keep all the sodas and liquor bottles stocked and in order. We had to take anything that was damaged along with other trash to the dumpster. In no time, we were drinking unlabeled bottles of wine coolers. Once we got used to those, we started drinking the harder liquor. We took some to our friends. I began to realize most of the guys were satisfied with far less alcohol than what I wanted. The alcohol began to take hold of me.

By the time I was 15, I was in trouble with the police. They sent me to a summer camp for young kids having trouble with alcohol. While at camp, I made my first vow—I won't be like my Dad or my Grandpa. I swore I wouldn't drink anymore. That settled that!

Unfortunately, the devil heard me, so my next temptation was to do drugs. I wasn't being like my dad, but the drugs soon had me spiraling downwards. My dad told me I wouldn't finish high school. To me, his words became a challenge to prove him wrong. I did finish high school but continued doing drugs and added drinking back into the mix. A month after graduation, I landed in prison for fighting under the influence of alcohol and drugs.

My girlfriend had a child while I was in prison. This is not the way to live your life with any kind of meaningful relationship. After sixteen months in the pen, I was free and went to work. I was doing well and then my drinking started again. In my mind, I was trying to escape the hopelessness that would not leave me. I knew how to pray, but there was some sort of blockage—I believe the devil implanted me with great shame. I felt I had no purpose in life, even with a small child I had fathered. For ten continuous years alcohol and drug related trouble ruled my life until I was sent to prison for the second time.

Looking back, I believe my broken relationships with women stemmed from the separation I had experienced from my mother at two. I truly didn't know how to relate to women for any length of time. The things I learned growing up were that "no one can be trusted," and "promises are made to be broken." How could I relate to and trust a woman with my messed up background? Could I be trusted?

I have learned to trust Jesus, and know that when He makes a promise, I can depend on Him to fulfill His word. He will not leave me or forsake me or anyone else. At this point, however, I still didn't know Him. I had another child and instead of being happy, I was upset with myself for bringing another baby into my life of chaos!

I ended up in prison for the third time because of drinking and drugs. I stepped over a line I supposedly had set for the drugs I used. It was like escalating into a dark hole of incomprehensible demoralization. I had no purpose, no direction, and no reason to be alive. I had my fortieth birthday in prison, a three time loser. Who cared?

God showed up in several people who provided me with books to read, such as *The Purpose Driven Life* by Rick Warren, and a picture Bible book. The pictures gave me understanding and helped me make sense of what I was reading in a regular Bible. One thing I saw in myself was that I had been in a personal wilderness for 40 years; **40 long years, wandering around like the Israelites.** I was extremely ready for my wanderings to come to an end!

I read in my Bible, "If you acknowledge and confess with your lips that Jesus is Lord and in your heart believe (adhere to, trust in, and rely on the truth) that God raised Him from the dead, you will be saved. For with the heart a person believes (adheres to, trusts in, and relies on Christ) and so is justified (declared righteous, acceptable to God), and with the mouth he confesses (declares openly and speaks out freely his faith) and confirms [his] salvation." (Romans 10:9, 10 AMPC)

When I finally understood this, I fell on my knees in my prison cell and asked the Lord Jesus Christ to forgive me of all my sin. His presence with me was real, and I immediately felt a glorious change inside of me. One of the first things He did for me was to help me be free from the many fears I had, probably because I had no security as a child. He showed me a verse in II Timothy 1:7, "You see, God has not given us a spirit of fear and timidity, but of power, love and self- discipline." (NLT)

I realized I did not need to be afraid of many things when Jesus was present. He cast those spirits away when I asked Him to enter my life. Part of my fear centered on trying to appear as a "macho man" when I was drinking. With Jesus, I no longer needed to show off or be a macho man.

Shortly after I came to Christ on my knees, I met a man who had already been in prison for fifty years with no chance of parole. He had come to Christ two years after he entered prison and had made it his mission to help others learn how to live for Jesus. This lifer got me a job in the DMV print shop where we had some time to talk.

One day, he asked me what music I was listening to. I told him Classical Rock. He told me I needed to be very careful what I was putting into my mind, because what you put in, is what will come out. He read, "Do not be conformed to this world, but be transformed by the renewing of your mind, that you may prove what is the good and acceptable and perfect will of God." (Romans 12:2)

That has proven to be a big help to me. I realize now if I start to have racing thoughts, the enemy of my soul is there to try to push me into drinking again or doing drugs. If you allow dark thoughts to come in, you can't be free. Satan will keep at you until you mess up. He doesn't want you to be out of his demonic control.

I came to understand, my grandfather, father, and I were all caught in the devil's clutch—he had us in a generational bondage, a stronghold of fear coupled with feelings of worthlessness. We each met our problems under the influence of alcohol. It supposedly gave us the ability to be cool about things, but I know for a fact, no one can make a wise decision with a pickled brain!

If you change your thinking, you can change your life. You can only change anything with the help of God, our heavenly Father. When He sees you are really interested in changing your ways by accepting His salvation made possible by His Son Jesus, He can open new doors for you.

I got out of prison for the third time, and had a new desire to please Him. I prayed for others in need. I was able to get a job and was doing well. When the company I was working for decided to cut back, God blessed me on my birthday. I was one of three who didn't get a pink slip. They then moved me to another state to help start up their business in a new place. This place has been good for me to get a new start away from the old haunts and old friends, jail, and facing death on drugs. These are the things that I struggled through while being a pawn of Satan.

I have a daughter named Serenity. I chose that name for her, hoping at the time, I had found serenity. Without the true forgiveness of my sins through the life-giving blood of Jesus, all my hope and wishing amounted to nothing. Jesus came to give all of us abundant life, but that life is only found in our relationship with Him. Real life worth living is when we surrender our hearts to Him, and He in turn fills our hearts with His overflowing love.

There is a prayer from Saint Francis of Assisi that is taught in Alcoholics Anonymous. It can change your heart and mind and bring peace about your past: "God grant me the serenity to accept the things I cannot change, courage to change the things I can, and wisdom to know the difference."

Repeat this often as you accept the forgiveness Jesus offers you. You will experience a deep cleansing change in your heart and a peace only He can give.

Young person, there is hope. You don't have to be a slave to fear or strongholds of addiction. Get on your knees and confess your sins before Jesus and believe in your heart He died for you. His Holy Spirit will guide you and help you continue to change. Then like me, you will know God loves you and you can share that love with others.

Surrender, listen, obey God—reap a life of joy and goodness. Come out of the darkness into the life your heart longs for. Don't waste 40 long years of your life in Satan's pit of continuous destruction and misery. You don't have to go to the bottom of the pit to get help. It is available for you now, if you will humble yourself and admit your need for a Savior, a Redeemer.

We are all sinners before a holy God, but He gives us the gift of eternal life when we choose to believe in His Son Jesus. In Him, we are able to be overcomers of all the dreaded sins that have plagued our lives. We are no longer slaves to the wicked works of darkness, but children of light; fully alive in Him, ready to stand in His presence.

THE QUEST FOR TRUTH IS IN EVERY GENERATION

If a television crew were to meet you on the street and ask you where someone could find truth, what would you say? Could you answer? Where do you think truth can be found? Do you even think a person can know the truth?

Young people everywhere take classes in high school and college that expose them to volumes of different social values and the philosophies men of the ages have espoused. Which one is really true? Each has a voice saying, "Follow me, I will show you the way to truth and happiness." A choice may be made to follow a visionary, but the happiness and idealistic outcomes never materialize. Young people end up in jail, disillusioned, broken or worse. Some die. The "truth" they followed was a lie. . . .

•

Some of the lies are the same in every generation. Satan's aim is to turn young hearts to rebellion that will cast off any moral standard they have been taught. Once he has them on this road, there is not much that will turn them around. I know; I have been there. Though I am of an older generation, the lies I hear being told to young people today are the very same ones I heard many years ago.

I grew up in a Reform Jewish family in New York City and attended our Sunday School until I was fifteen. I loved learning Old Testament stories and memorized the Ten Commandments. My father believed in God, but my mother wasn't sure. Nevertheless, we were proud of our heritage.

At the tender age of sixteen, I went away to college during the time of anti-war marches, sit-ins, marijuana, psychedelic rock music, and some influential Marxist professors. *Time* magazine even ran a story that asked, "Is God Dead?" Moral absolutes were giving way to, "It's my body, I can do what I want."

My worldview was shaped, therefore, by these radical times. I am glad for the peaceful Civil Rights movement which brought about needed change in our nation, but otherwise these changes were disruptive to a free society. I graduated with no solid goals in mind and returned to New York City. I found part-time work in a department store and decided to take studio art classes.

Many of my generation were searching for truth and peace, so we turned to Eastern Religion and the occult. A few years after college, I found myself living in a hippie commune in New Mexico, near the Pueblo Indian reservation. They had "church" meetings in a tepee where they ate the hallucinogenic plant, peyote, but prayed in Jesus' name. Hmm, my searching heart took note of that name.

On a trip to Berkeley one summer, I noticed a poster on a street-light that said, "Jews for Jesus." What? How can that be? But the thought rested in my heart.

Back at the commune, I went for a pregnancy test one Friday afternoon and it was positive. Reality began to set in. This was before Roe v. Wade, but abortion was legal in New Mexico. The kind woman at the clinic said to think about what to do over the weekend. I visited a friend who had a young child and she told me that having a baby was a very spiritual experience. Since that is what I hungered for, I was at peace. The father did not want to help with our child nor did I particularly want that. This "free love" was neither free nor was it love.

A few months after the birth of my beautiful baby, I traveled to Hawaii with another single mom and her child. We lived in a makeshift shelter in a small commune, practically sleeping under the stars. Little did we know that the Jesus Movement was in full force on the island. However, I didn't catch on right away. Yet God was at work. There was a Bible there and one day I opened it to Isaiah 54:5, "For thy maker is thine husband, the Lord of hosts is His name; and thy Redeemer the Holy One of Israel; the God of the whole earth shall He be called." (KJV) Wow! This was great comfort to me.

Driving with some friends one afternoon, we picked up a hitchhiker who seemed kind of weird. From the back seat he asked, "Have you ever asked Jesus into your heart?"

The next day as I was "meditating,"—a habit from Eastern religion—I did ask Jesus into my heart, though I didn't understand what it meant. I figured that it couldn't hurt. I was doing what the young man suggested. No one seemed to argue or care about it.

The Hare Krishna's had love feasts on the island where we danced and chanted. I thought this might be the way to peace and truth. The god, Krishna, was a man, and that concept opened my mind to the possibility that God could become a man—most definitely not a Jewish concept. I almost joined them but at the end of the love feast I went down to the beach, dove into the water, and decided I'd go to the Christian meeting the next evening to which a friend had invited me.

I had met a few new Christian friends over the months, and they were glowing with joy and freedom. They said they would read the Bible and do what it said, and it was absolutely wonderful!

So, at the Christian meeting in a coffee shack, I repented for my sins and prayed to receive Jesus. Everything changed. The New Age thinking that had filled my darkened mind, the idea that you are one with the cosmos, gave way to the reality that God is the Creator, and I am one of His creations, loved by Him.

The peace and truth I had been searching for was found in a relationship with Jesus. The Jesus Movement was not a traditional church. We went to meetings, worshiped and were taught the Bible. God's Word and our close knit fellowship filled me up. No more wondering or wandering. The One who is the Way, the Truth, and the Life was in my heart and life. We sang, "I have decided to follow Jesus, no turning back. . ." And now more than fifty years later, that is still my song. . . .

•

Do you listen to songs that fill you with joy? Or is your mind feasting on the lies and darkness of the devil sung by another troubled soul? Come to the true light that has been sent to deliver you from that dark domain. Only Jesus can shut down the devil's voice in your mind. There is no other source of power that can deliver you from his grip, mentally or spiritually. Having done this, you will then know why *Jesus truly is the Way to the Father, the source of Truth, and real Life.* (John 14:6 KJV italics added)

REJOICE

*I love the Lord, because He has heard
my voice and my supplications.
Because He has inclined His ear to me,
I will call on Him as long as I live.*

*The cords and sorrows of death were
around me, and the terrors of Sheol (the
place of the dead) had laid hold of me; I
suffered anguish and grief (trouble
and sorrow).*

*Then I called upon the name of the Lord:
"O Lord, I beseech You, save my life
and deliver me!'*

*Gracious is the Lord, and [rigidly] righteous:
yes, our God is merciful.
The Lord preserves the simple; I was
brought low, and He helped and
saved me.*

*Return to your rest, O my soul, for the Lord
has dealt bountifully with you.
For You have delivered my life from death,
my eyes from tears, and my feet from
stumbling and falling.
I will walk before the Lord in the land of the
living.*

*Psalm 116:1-9
Amplified Bible*

A prayer to confess sins and receive Christ Jesus, the only Son of God, as your Savior.

I come to You, holy God, my heavenly Father, to ask for Your forgiveness for all my sins.

I understand and recognize my sins have not been done in a vacuum, but have been against You. I ask forgiveness for:
--disparaging Your holy name and Your very existence.

–things I have said, raising my fist in pride against You.

–going my own way and turning from Your love and goodness.

–the sins caused by the lusts of my flesh.

–sins against my parents, even if they were not following You themselves.

–sins against others.

For all these and more, I ask Your forgiveness and willingly turn from my past life of darkness. I believe Jesus died to pay the penalty for my sins, but You then raised Him from the dead. He will give me life that breaks the power of sin. I can walk in His righteousness to His honor. By receiving His life, I am a new creation. He will cleanse my heart of sin so that I can become Your child. Help me grow in my understanding of Your salvation. (Finish with your own prayer of confession of sins that come to mind.) End with thankfulness and praise for the mercy and grace He has shown to you through His forgiveness. Amen.

READ AFTER PRAYING
I John 1:5-10

This is the message which we have heard from Him and declare to you, that God is light. And in Him there is no darkness at all.

If we say that we have fellowship with Him and walk in darkness, we lie and do not practice the truth.

But if we walk in the light, as He is in the light, we have fellowship with one another, and the blood of Jesus Christ His Son, cleanses us from all sin.

But if we say we have no sin, we deceive ourselves, and the truth is not in us.

But if we confess our sins, He is faithful and just to forgive us our sins, and to cleanse us from all unrighteousness.

If we say we have not sinned, we make Him a liar, and His word is not in us.

New King James Version

End Notes

Undoubtedly, there are many additional stories which could be told. These true accounts only touch the tip of the iceberg in the scope of sin and destruction a person can experience. The current wave of changing lifestyles and online temptations, are other avenues of Satan's design to lure the unsuspecting into eternal destruction. No matter how innocent things may seem, the enslavement is lurking in the shadows.

Though there were some contacts who had interest in helping others avoid dark choices, the retelling of their stories was too troubling to their souls to bring the evil forth. As with soldiers who have been in a war, they would say, "War is hell and I don't want to talk about it!" Why glorify the works of darkness? Sin leads to hell. Don't doubt it!

Closing thoughts from God's Word:

Colossians 2:8 "Beware, lest anyone cheat you through philosophy and empty deceit, according to the tradition of men, according to the principles of the world and not according to Christ."

II Corinthians 6:1,2 "As God's fellow workers, then, we urge you not to receive God's grace in vain. For He says: "In the time of favor I heard you, and in the day of salvation I helped you." Behold now is the time of favor; now is the day of salvation!" (NLT)

Hebrews 2:1-3 "We must pay closer attention, therefore, to what we have heard, so that we do not drift away. For if the message spoken by angles was binding, and every transgression and disobedience received its just punishment, how shall we escape if we neglect such a great salvation?" (NLT)

Ephesians 4:23-25 "And be constantly renewed in the spirit of your mind [having a fresh mental and spiritual attitude]. And put on the new nature (the regenerate self) created in God's image, [Godlike] in true righteousness and holiness. Therefore, reject all falsity and being done with it, let everyone express the truth with his neighbor, for we are all parts of one body and members of one another." (AMPC)

Matthew 7:13, 14 "Enter by the narrow gate; for wide is the gate and broad is the way that leads to destruction, and there are many who go in by it. Because narrow is the gate and difficult is the way which leads to life, and there are few who find it."

Matthew 6:33 "Seek first the kingdom of God and His righteousness, and all these things shall be added to you."

Psalm 16:11 "You will show me the path of life: in Your presence is fullness of joy; at Your right hand are pleasures forever more."

I John 5:13 These things I have written to you who believe in the Son of God, that you may know you have eternal life, and *continue* to believe on the name of the Son of God.

☙❧☙❧☙❧☙

A happy day came for the "Son of Disobedience," when he married "Lowest of the Low." As in all marriages there have been some hard adjustments. However, they are earnestly growing in their oneness of spirit. They desire to be *trophies of God's grace*, as they show forth the love and forgiveness He has extended into their lives through salvation in Jesus Christ alone.

About the Author

Paula Cole has been married over fifty years and is the mother of three, and the grandmother to eleven special blessings. In her career, she taught children of all ages in both schools and churches. Her testimony includes a near death experience, after which God called her to take a deeper step in her commitment and relationship to Him. Her favorite scriptures together are Philippians 4:13 and John 15:5b: "I can do all things through Christ who strengthens me. . . .Without Him, I can do nothing."

www.ingramcontent.com/pod-product-compliance
Lightning Source LLC
Chambersburg PA
CBHW072108290426
44110CB00014B/1870